The New York Times

POCKET
MBA
SERIES

D1562720

BUSINESS PLANNING
25 KEYS TO A SOUND BUSINESS PLAN

EDWARD E. WILLIAMS, PH.D.
JAMES R. THOMPSON, PH.D.
H. ALBERT NAPIER, PH.D.
Rice University

Lebhar-Friedman Books
NEW YORK • CHICAGO • LOS ANGELES • LONDON • PARIS • TOKYO

For *The New York Times*
Mike Levitas, Editorial Director, Book Development
Tom Redburn, General Series Editor
Brent Bowers, Series Editor
James Schembari, Series Editor

Lebhar-Friedman Books
425 Park Avenue
New York, NY 10022

Published by Lebhar-Friedman Books
Lebhar-Friedman Books is a company of Lebhar-Friedman Inc.

Printed in the United States of America

Library of Congress Cataloging-in-Publication Data
On file at Library of Congress
ISBN 0-86730-775-7

DESIGN & PRODUCTION BY MILLER WILLIAMS DESIGN ASSOCIATES

Visit our Web site at lfbooks.com

Volume Discounts

This book makes a great human resources training reference.
Call (212) 756-5240 for information on volume discounts.

INTRODUCTION

LEBHAR-FRIEDMAN BOOKS is proud to present *The New York Times* Pocket MBA Series, 12 invaluable reference volumes that are easily accessible to all businesspersons, from first level managers to the executive suite. The books are written by Ph.D.s who teach in the MBA programs in some of the finest schools in the country. A team of business editors from *The New York Times*—Mike Levitas, Tom Redburn, Brent Bowers, and James Schembari—provided their own expertise to edit a reference series that is beyond compare.

The New York Times Pocket MBA Series offers quick-reference key points learned in top MBA programs. The 25-key structure of each volume presents an unparalleled synopsis of crucial principles of specific areas of business expertise. The unique approach to this series packages academic books for consumers in an easy-to-use trade format that is ideal for the individual businessperson as well as an excellent training reference manual. Be sure to get all 12 titles in the series to complete your own MBA education.

Joseph Mills
Senior Managing Editor
Lebhar-Friedman Books

The New York Times Pocket MBA
Series includes these 12 volumes:

25 KEYS TO A SOUND BUSINESS PLAN

C O N T E N T S

KEY 1

Every business should have a mission

Creating and planning a business is not easy, but the task can be approached in a systematic way that will maximize the probability of success. First, it should be recognized that every business has to have a reason for its existence. Second, every entrepreneur should know why his or her new business should come into being. Entrepreneurs start new businesses for lots of reasons, some good and some not so good. Many entrepreneurs simply want freedom and independence from the work place. Unfortunately, the market place may be more demanding than the most meticulous boss, and the entrepreneur who starts a business just to get away from the constraints of a job may be sorely disappointed.

It is not unusual for entrepreneurs to want a creative opportunity, and they embark on a new business as a means of self-expression. This motivation for owning and operating an enterprise is certainly acceptable, but in the final analysis

Perpetual devotion to what a man calls his business, is only to be sustained by perpetual neglect of many other things.

Robert Louis Stevenson, **An Apology for Idlers**

few businesses are deemed successful unless they make money, and for good reason: Few entities can exist for long if they do not become profitable at some point.

The simple desire to have a business is not sufficient to justify the existence of an enterprise. Even the desire to make a profit is not sufficient for a business to succeed. There also has to be an economic explanation for a firm to thrive. A business must produce goods and services that people will buy in sufficient quantities to justify producing those goods and services. The entrepreneur who says, "I want to be in the catering business in San

Diego because I am a good cook and I like the climate in San Diego," may not be in business very long if nobody buys his or her food. Unfortunately, there are a lot of reasons people don't buy things. The price has to be right. Quality is a consideration. What else is on the market is a factor. You may be the best cook in San Diego, but if you can't sell your food at a reasonable price, you will probably not succeed. Also, if you can't deliver on time and can't provide a tasteful setting for your meals, your business will not endure.

The successful business comes into being and survives because a smart entrepreneur has identified a real demand for specific goods and/or services. Furthermore, the demand must be satisfied by being able to sell those goods and/or services at a price people can afford. Finally, the demand must be met with a cost structure that will yield a sufficient profit to justify the investment in time, energy and money that must be made by the entrepreneur and his backers (financial and otherwise).

Given the caveats outlined above, it should be obvious that the first thing an entrepreneur should do when he is contemplating establishing a new business (or continuing an existing one) is to determine why that business should exist. It is smart to spell out the reasons in a short narrative statement that reflects the motivations of both the entrepreneur and the market served. This narrative statement is called an enterprise mission. A possible mission statement might be: "The ABC Company wishes to provide X (for the product and/or service area where the business will be, or currently is, located) with the highest quality Y (the product and/or service being provided), while permitting the owner(s) of the business to achieve personal and financial independence."

KEY 2

Every business needs to define what the business does and identify a market opportunity

It may seem simple to define what a business does, but it often isn't. For example, a company named Service Corporation International, or S.C.I., thought it was a funeral-home chain. The company believed it provided funeral services for and buried dead people. S.C.I., started in 1962 in Houston, Texas by an entrepreneur named Robert Waltrip, soon discovered that what the firm *really* did was provide a secondary market for people who wanted to sell their family funeral homes and cemeteries. Of course, the operating part of the business was important and the businesses bought by S.C.I. had to continue to provide good funeral services and bury the dead. But the real success of the company (which went from about $100,000 in revenues in 1962 to about $3 billion in 1998) was in its acquisition achievements.

The agreed-upon business definition should be comprehensive enough to encourage creative thinking but also constricted enough to provide direction for the company. The fact that S.C.I.

provided funeral services and owned cemeteries was insufficient to define the nature of the enterprise. Even a more comprehensive definition that recognized that the real purpose of funeral homes and cemeteries was to provide services and merchandise related to the care and dispositions of the dead was not sufficient. A more adequate definition also had to recognize that what funeral homes and cemeteries actually did was provide assistance to families who did not wish to take care of the unpleasant details associated with memorializing and burying the dead. In SCI's case, it also had to take into account the fact that the growth and development of the business depended on locating and purchasing, on reasonable terms, family businesses that could not easily be sold to outsiders.

Over time, companies may change their business definition, and this may lead to new opportunities. In the energy industry, for example, most oil companies once thought of themselves as drillers, or refiners, or marketers of oil and gas products (or perhaps all three). Today, most of these companies consider themselves as energy companies that provide oil, gas, electricity, coal, solar energy and other forms of energy. By the same token, S.C.I. has refined its business definition in a way that has allowed it to develop a creative approach to marketing a service that has typically been unmarketable. By selling pre-need contracts for future services, S.C.I. locations throughout the world have enabled consumers to make rational, unemotional decisions (to the customers' advantage) and has locked in future business for the company.

The business environment has become more complex and competitive, forcing many firms to broaden their business definition. For example, individual banks have formed bank holding companies and are becoming more like general financial-services companies. Newspapers are recognizing that they are in the communications business rather than just publishing. Stock brokerage businesses are becoming financial-services companies. Industries that broadened their business scope have had more growth and development than industries that have clung to historical business definitions. For example, the steel industry has not been particularly imaginative and has experienced slower growth than those industries that have enlarged their business scope. In specifying the mission statement and defining the business, the entrepreneur must ascertain if there is a need for the business. The following questions must be answered for new enterprises:

◆ Why should the company be started?

◆ What unique niche will it fill?

◆ Why hasn't another business already filled the niche?

If a business already exists, the entrepreneur must ascertain the following:

◆ Why was the firm started in the first place? What niche has it been filling?

◆ What competition exists and why does it exist?

Whether the firm is a start-up or already exists, the entrepreneur must prepare a market analysis. The entrepreneur can complete the market analysis or hire a market-analysis consulting company to prepare it. Key economic, geographic, demographic and other relevant data will be needed.

KEY 3

The entrepreneur must identify the external factors that may have an impact on the business

After completing the market analysis, the entrepreneur must identify the external factors over which he may have no control. Current data on these non-controllable variables must be gathered and analyzed. The entrepreneur might ask the question, Where do I get information on external variables? Fortunately, a lot of data is available and for surprisingly little cost. First, numerous government publications provide a significant amount of information. These publications are inexpensive and are available at U.S. Government bookstores located across the country. Almost everything the government prints is available through these stores.

One important source of information is the *Statistical Abstract*. This government document includes a wide variety of factual and statistical data that appear in simplified, abstract form. It also includes references indicating the source of the original information that the entrepreneur may be able to use for more extensive research and analysis. The cost of the *Statistical Abstract*, which is published annually, is about $50 for a paperback version.

Every five years a census is taken that gathers data on sales, employees, payroll and a variety of other data for almost every business category. Many previous editions of this publication, known as the *Census of Business*, are available. Entrepreneurs may be able to use this historic information to determine long-term trends for businesses in which they have an interest. Similarly, entrepreneurs may find the population census taken at the beginning of each decade to be helpful. For many types of businesses, demographic data (population, age groupings, income levels) are important and can be obtained for small areas called census tracts. The local Chamber of Commerce is another excellent source of economic, statistical and other information as is the economics department of many large banks.

Another first-rate government source of data is the *U.S. Industry and Trade Outlook*, which is published annually by the Department of Commerce. This publication provides information on virtually every American industry and includes forecasts. For those entrepreneurs interested in economic data such as gross domestic product (G.D.P.), consumer price indexes and interest rates. *The Economic Report of the President* is mandatory reading. The Small Business Administration is yet another great source of information. The S.B.A. provides booklets on topics such as establishing accounting systems and product pricing for free or at a nominal cost.

In business, one certain thing is taxes. The Internal Revenue Service, as well as state comptrollers' offices, can provide tax assistance and tax guide materials for business owners. For news about national and international business events and trends, the *Wall Street Journal* and *The New York Times* are indispensible. Other valuable business publications include *BusinessWeek*, *Forbes* and *Fortune*. And *The Economist* is a must-read for anybody who wants to understand the global economy.

Earlier in our history, what happened in distant countries such as Yugoslavia and Iraq did not have much impact on the United States. Today, international dislocations, such as reductions in energy production and distribution, can affect a business.

Clearly, the entrepreneur cannot identify and analyze all the information he will need. However, an informed business owner must know what to read and how to read it quickly to get information pertinent to his business. This ability is an important aspect of managing and planning a business. Many businesses probably started as a result of something read by an entrepreneur.

October. This is one of the peculiarly dangerous months to speculate stocks in. The others are July, January, September, April, November, May, March, June, December, August, and February.

Mark Twain,
Pudd'nhead Wilson's Calendar

KEY 4

Business success depends on analyzing the nature and contemplating the future of the business

After determining the most significant external factors having an impact on the business and locating sources of information about those factors, the entrepreneur must analyze the nature and contemplate the future of the business. If the data exist, the entrepreneur should utilize projections about external factors that have already been made by experts. The entrepreneur might make some adjustments based on her assessment of the situation. For example, the prognostications of various economists might be used as a starting point for compiling macroeconomic statistics that are important for a given business. Forecasts of economic data such as gross domestic product, consumer prices, interest rates and other such items made by economists appear regularly in business publications. Although economic forecasts frequently vary (and, in fact, economists sometimes have heated debates with one another about them), such forecasts are probably better than any seat-of-the-pants opinions of entrepreneurs who have never studied economics. Even so, the entrepreneur's judgment must play the deciding role. The entrepreneur must be convinced that the expert's forecasts are relevant to her situation.

In contemplating the future of the business, the entrepreneur has numerous sources of data. For example, the *U.S. Industry and Trade Outlook* that was mentioned earlier is a useful resource. Another governmental agency that gathers and interprets data is the United States Department of Labor. This organization prepares helpful forecasts on variables such as the labor force and price trends. For a smaller firm that operates in a limited geographic area, however, these national forecasts may be of little assistance. Local area economic variables should be analyzed. Fortunately, local banks and the Chambers of Commerce in larger cities can be consulted. These organizations often create and maintain data files and projections for important economic, demographic and competitive conditions in their communities.

The entrepreneur may not have to reinvent the wheel to initiate a business. There are existing consulting and data-analysis companies that assemble information and make projections about important statistical series. Spending a few thousand dollars with an expert consultant to analyze and make projections for important external factors may be a good investment. Even if the entrepreneur has the expertise, it will probably take less time for the outside organization to gather and analyze the relevant data.

Another source of consulting assistance may be available by hiring an economics or business school professor. These individuals can provide exceptional services at reasonable rates because much of their overhead expenses, such as office space and clerical assistance, are already covered. In addition, many of these individuals have students who are smart and can carry out assignments given to them by the professors. Students usually work at remarkably low rates and are often the same individuals hired by the consulting companies a year later. At that juncture, their compensation is much higher (even though the work is similar) because their salaries are greater and the consulting firm has a large built-in overhead factor.

KEY 5

The business idea determines the key factors that result in business success

After analyzing the nature and contemplating the future of the business, the entrepreneur must determine the key internal factors that affect successful performance. These factors may differ in various industries. For example, the sales-growth rate may be the most important element for companies with some degree of market control. An aggressive sales promotion and advertising program may be the way to success in this case. In more competitive situations, adopting an aggressive selling strategy may not be helpful in gaining a larger market share. For example, companies may have prices dictated to them by larger competitors or by customers who have an important market position. In this situation, the key internal factors may be cost control and efficiency of operations.

Every business has its own unique set of key internal factors. In the manufacturing industry, inventory turnover, product-rejection rates, equipment downtime and plant capacity are typically important. If a business is services-oriented, then control of overhead expenses, labor costs and accounts-receivable management are important. Owners of retail firms must focus on markup percentages, inventory management and promotional activities. Those organizations having high fixed costs need to pay close attention to factors such as dollar and unit break-even points and their cost structure (issues that will be discussed later).

There are several internal variables that influence risk encountered by the firm. The most important of these factors is the predictability of business revenues. Business planning is much easier if the entrepreneur can forecast revenue with some degree of confidence for several years. Accuracy of revenue expectation is important so the entrepreneur can avoid financial embarrassment in arranging disbursements. Even when the revenue pattern is volatile over a period of time, if the entrepreneur understands the nature of the volatility, then he can use this information in his planning to reduce the impact of fluctuations. When revenues are volatile and unpredictable, even the planning process cannot reduce the impact of variability.

Never fear the want of business. A man who qualifies himself well for his calling, never fails of employment.

Thomas Jefferson, Writings

KEY 6

The major strengths of the business should be identified in detail

The next step in creating a business is to outline the primary strengths of the business that provide the impetus for a successful venture. What are these strengths? They may vary from business to business. For some enterprises, it will be the creation of a new product for which there is no competitive option. In others, it may be selling a comparable product at a lower price. Providing better service or a higher quality product may be the primary strength of some business ventures.

The entrepreneur can be a key asset to a business. The individual's knowledge, expertise and overall energy level may be the most important success factor to an enterprise. George Ballas, the famous entrepreneur who invented the WeedEater™, used to say that the most important determinant for the success of a business was the burning desire of the entrepreneur to succeed. With that desire, even a relatively weak business idea might be turned into a success. Without it, even the best idea might be doomed to failure.

In some situations, the lack of expertise and entrepreneurial attitude of the competition may provide the major strength of a business. Typically, the more established a firm is in an industry, the more likely the firm tends to become conservative, fat, dumb, comfortable and lazy. Such situations provide the opportunity for a new entrepreneur who will go the extra mile and provide better service or a superior product.

Sometimes the primary strength of a business is its marketing strategy. The entrepreneur or some person employed in the business may have created an outstanding advertising program, or organized a larger distributor network, or determined a unique niche in a highly specialized market. The business location sometimes plays an important role. Just as in real-estate purchases, there is a saying in marketing that there are three reasons for the success of a retail establishment: location, location, location. Selling may be a key ingredient. It has been said that behind every successful entrepreneur there is a super salesperson. Usually, that person is the entrepreneur!

Other strengths of a business may be found among the following factors:

- The financial capacity of the enterprise

- The firm's ability to grant credit terms to customers

- The lack of indebtedness or other fixed obligations of the business

- The cost effectiveness and efficiency of the plant and equipment

- The age of the plant and equipment

- The employees who work for the firm

- The lack of a union among the employees

- Existing contracts or the promise of contracts from major customers

- The financial condition of the clients of the business

- The general economic climate

KEY 7

The major weaknesses of the business should also be identified in detail

One of the most important steps in creating and planning a business for an entrepreneur is to specify the major weaknesses of the business. Why? Because it is usually these weaknesses that cause a business to fail.

In many situations, the process of outlining the weaknesses is the reverse of specifying the strengths. Here are some questions the entrepreneur can ask to ascertain weaknesses:

◆ Is the product or service really very different from other products or services available in the market? If not, this lack of differentiation may be a fatal weakness.

◆ Is there so much competition that it may be impossible to create a unique niche in the market place? If so, the lack of a niche may also be an important weakness.

◆ Is it possible to find the right location? If a
good location cannot be found, this may be
a major weakness for a business that sells
to the general public.

For many new organizations, the primary weaknesses center around the newness itself. Potential
customers just may not realize that you are in
business. An aggressive marketing strategy can
help the entrepreneur overcome their lack of
awareness. It takes time and can be costly for
entrepreneurs to build relationships with suppliers
so that the company can become an established
and trusted customer and get preferred treatment.
Furthermore, the initial employees of the new
company may not have the skills or experience
that are needed to keep production, distribution
and selling problems at acceptable levels. As the
firm ages, these problems can be resolved, but the
new company must have sufficient financial
resources to keep going while improvements are
made.

Typically, one of the major weaknesses of new
companies relates to financial factors. The business may not have enough capital. Sometimes the
optimistic business owner, who thought the firm
would reach the break-even sales point in a short
time period, has underestimated the financial
requirements of the organization. When a new
venture starts operations with a lot of borrowed
capital, just paying the interest on the debt may be
an issue. Initially, it can be difficult for a new
organization to obtain credit from suppliers. In
such situations, the supplier may require the
entrepreneur to pay cash on delivery (C.O.D.)
until the company is more established and has
built a good payment history.

Without some dissimulation no business can be carried on at all.

Lord Chesterfield, letter to his son

KEY 8

A complete business plan should be prepared

A complete business plan should be prepared that provides a description of the industry, the form and organizational structure of the company, *pro forma* financial statements, a strategic plan and an operating plan. The actual preparation of a business plan is beyond the scope of this book. However, the entrepreneur must realize the importance of completing the planning process and the writing of a business plan. The analysis specified earlier in this book will provide much of the information required to complete the business plan outline that follows. For readers who would like to see a more complete treatment of how to prepare a business plan, we recommend the following: *Entrepreneurship and Productivity*, Chapters 5 and 6, by Edward E. Williams and James R. Thompson (University Press of America, 1998).

BUSINESS PLAN OUTLINE

I. Executive Summary
   A. A one-paragraph statement about the nature of the business.
   B. A one-paragraph rationale for the existence of the business.
   C. A brief statement about the financing required.
   D. Key characteristics of the industry.
   E. Structure and important features of the company.

II. Complete Analysis of the Industry

III. Form and Organizational Structure of the Company

IV. *Pro Forma* Financial Statements
   A. Balance sheet at inception.
   B. Income, cash flow and balance sheet *pro forma* statements over the planning horizon.

V. The Strategic Plan
   A. Statement of the enterprise mission.
   B. Definition of the business.
   C. Specific enterprise goals.
   D. Enterprise strategies.
   E. Statement of planning premises.
   F. Strategic long-range plan objectives.
         1. Sales, cost and profit projections.
         2. Major capital additions (plant, equipment, etc.).
         3. Cash flow and financing.
         4. Personnel requirements.

VI. The Operating Plan
   A. Marketing (sales) plan.
   B. Production plan.
   C. Various expense plans.
   D. Operating income plan.
   E. Cash flow and cash balance plans.
   F. Planned balance sheet.
   G. Planned operating and financial ratios.

VII. Appendices
   A. Pertinent contracts.
   B. Technical information.
   C. Other supporting data.

KEY 9

The business plan should be specific and well written

The business plan should be specific and well written. It should begin with an executive summary that answers several important questions:

◆ What is the business all about?

◆ Who are the key people involved in the business venture?

◆ Where is the business located (if it is relevant)?

◆ Why is there a need for the company to exist?

The executive summary should also include the following information:

◆ A succinct statement of the enterprise mission and definition of the nature of the business.

- ◆ A description of what financing is required and how the funds will be utilized.

- ◆ An outline of the primary characteristics of the business in which the venture will operate or in which it already operates.

- ◆ A discussion of the salient features of the venture.

In the executive summary, the entrepreneur must focus on the important external factors that may influence the business, key features of the specific business venture, and the financing of the enterprise.

A complete, detailed analysis of the industry in which the proposed venture operates should constitute the second section of a business plan. An in-depth research and analysis effort should be completed. This effort should include principal industry characteristics (economic, social, demographic and political) and a summary. Industry data may be obtained from the sources mentioned earlier. The Internal Revenue Service now requires every type of business to adopt a Principal Business Activity Code. These codes are based on the North American Industry Classification System. Thus, every business has an N.A.I.C.S. code. The census of business data (mentioned earlier) is gathered every five years.

These data allow the entrepreneur to obtain industry information on items such as sales, number of employees and industry structure by N.A.I.C.S. code. The entrepreneur can also use the forecasts and projections included in the Department of Commerce's *U.S. Industry and Trade Outlook* that is available at most U.S. Government bookstores. Since most industries have trade associations, the entrepreneur can also obtain data from these organizations. Information available can vary from specific studies completed by economists and others and from large companies in the industry. A thorough library research project on the industry the entrepreneur intends to enter should be completed as one of the principal parts of the business planning process.

The next section of the business plan should include an outline of the form and organizational structure of the proposed business venture. This effort will assist the entrepreneur in determining how many employees will be necessary during the planning period. Potential investors in the business will also be interested in the organizational structure. In fact, the people in the business venture are often the most important determinants of its success. For this reason, venture capitalists and bankers will often provide financial resources based on their confidence in the people rather than in the industry outlook and the financial *pro forma* statements.

As we said earlier, while good business venture ideas are important, they must have a specific form and be executed well to be successful. Because people play such a critical role in the success of an enterprise, the section on organization is a good place to include the resumes of the principals of the business. The next section of the business plan should include *pro forma* financial statements. The first statement prepared should be the opening *pro forma* balance sheet. This statement should specify the asset and liability position of the business venture at the day operations commence. If the firm is already operating, the statement should reflect the condition of the business at the beginning of the planning period. The balance sheet includes categories to which the financial commitments are allocated (assets) and categories indicating where the funds are obtained to finance the enterprise (liabilities).

Pro forma income and cash flow statements should also be prepared. These statements are a result of the planning process. Each value included is determined by starting with an initial forecast number that is subsequently refined based on the enterprises objectives. Therefore, the *pro forma* statements are based on the strategic and operating plans that follow next in the business plan (see detailed discussion in following keys).

When the business plan has been completed, the entrepreneur must consider various presentation methods. First, it should be recognized that all plans are subject to change depending upon circumstances and the passage of time. What was a reasonable plan last month may no longer be reasonable today. Therefore the business plan should be kept in a loose-leaf binder format so that it can be updated on an "as required" basis. Plans prepared for outside investors (such as venture capitalists) may be placed in professional looking, bound volumes that create a favorable impression and cause the reader to want to find out more about the opportunity.

Dispatch is the soul of business, and nothing contributes more to dispatch than method. Lay down a method for everything and stick to it inviolably, as far as unexpected incidents may follow.

Lord Chesterfield, letter to his son

KEY 10

Financial statements are the heart of the business plan

---

ro forma financial statements are the heart of the business plan. They include the hard numbers to which the entrepreneur must commit if the business is to be successful. The first statement prepared should be the opening *pro forma* balance sheet. This statement should specify the asset and liability position of the business venture on the day operations commence. If the firm is already operating, the statement should reflect the condition of the enterprise at the beginning of the planning period. The balance sheet includes categories to which the financial commitments are allocated (assets) and categories indicating where the funds are obtained to finance the enterprise (liabilities).

A *pro forma* income statement, cash flow analysis and balance sheet should also be prepared for every year in the planning period. Detailed projections of revenues, expense items, expected profits, debt service, cash flow, assets and liabilities should be made. Footnotes to the statements should be provided to explain the assumptions behind each number.

A *pro forma* balance sheet for the ABC Company appears as follows:

ABC Company, Inc. *Pro Forma* Balance Sheet
January 1, 2000

Assets		Liabilities	
Cash	$110,000	Note payable	$150,000
Inventory	5,000	Stockholders equity	100,000
Furniture,fixtures			
and equipment	75,000		
Leasehold improvements	60,000		
	$250,000		$250,000

Pro forma income and cash flow statements for future years 2000 to 2004 are indicated below:

ABC Company, Inc. *Pro Forma* Income and Cash Flow
2000–2004

	2000	2001	2002	2003	2004
Sales	$400,000	$500,000	$600,000	$700,000	$800,000
Cost of sales	320,000	400,000	480,000	560,000	640,000
Operating income	80,000	100,000	120,000	140,000	160,000
Interest expense	15,000	15,000	15,000	15,000	15,000
Income before taxes	65,000	85,000	105,000	125,000	145,000
Income taxes	10,000	20,000	25,000	30,000	35,000
Net income	55,000	65,000	80,000	95,000	110,000
Add depreciation	27,000	27,000	27,000	27,000	27,000
Net cash flow	$82,000	$92,000	$107,000	$122,000	$137,000

Pro forma statements are a result of the planning process. Each value included is determined by starting with an initial forecast number that is subsequently refined based on the objectives of the enterprise. Therefore, the *pro forma* statements are based on the strategic and operating plans that follow in the business plan (in Key 11). To properly prepare the *pro forma* balance sheet and the *pro forma* income and cash flow statements, the entrepreneur will probably need to utilize an accountant.

KEY 11

A strategic plan should be developed to determine what products or services the business is going to offer

A strategic plan should be developed to determine what products or services the business is going to offer and to which customers they will be offered. Geographic areas should also be specified. The broad goals for the organization are included in the strategic plan that typically includes several years as its planning horizon. The following items are usually part of the strategic plan:

- ◆ The mission statement of the business

- ◆ A listing of goals for the enterprise

- ◆ The strategies that need to be developed in order to accomplish the goals

- ◆ A statement of the planning premises

An example of a strategic plan follows.

STRATEGIC PLAN EXAMPLE

Definition of the Business:

The ABC Company will be a full-service car wash providing service and merchandise related to the care and cleaning of automobiles and trucks in the area surrounding Highland Park, New Jersey.

Enterprise Goals:

1. To provide the highest quality car and truck cleaning services.
2. To be recognized as an honorable and ethical firm.
3. To provide the proprietor of the business with personal and financial independence and pride in a service well performed.
4. To earn a fair rate of return for the investors in the business.

Enterprise Strategies:

1. To price our merchandise and services at a fair and competitive level.
2. To achieve optimum long-term profitable growth in order to establish a leadership position among the car-care firms in Highland Park.
3. To hire and train competent people.
4. To develop and maintain an organization whose conduct at all levels and at all times justifies the trust of the community.
5. To recognize and reward our employees according to their abilities and contributions.

Statement of Planning Premises:

1. We shall have our required financing in place by Dec. 1, 1999.
2. We shall be able to hire eight qualified employees prior to opening.
3. We shall be able to lease our location and be operating by Jan. 1, 2000.

KEY 12

An operating plan should be prepared to determine how to run the business effectively

Another important part of the business plan is the operating plan for the business. The operating plan specifies how the business will be developed in the months or year ahead. The operating plan should include the following items:

- A marketing (sales) plan

- A manufacturing plan

- Various expense plans

- An operating income plan

- Cash flow and cash balance plans

- A planned balance sheet

- A financial plan

- Planned operating and financial ratios

ABC Company Operating Plan
for the Year 2000

Marketing (Sales) Budget:

Sales (100/day @ $8)	$292,000
Other merchandise	108,000
	$400,000

Production Budget:

Car wash process data indicate that at no time should we have to worry about peak-load demand problems. There may be some days when we handle as many as 200 car washes per day, and we have the capacity to perform these without inconveniencing our customers.

Merchandise Expense Budget:

Merchandise should cost about 50 percent of what it is sold for. That is, we shall mark up our own merchandise sold to twice cost.

Personnel Salaries and Fringes Budget:

General Manager	$40,000
Assistant Manager	36,000
Attendants 5 @ $10,000	50,000
Clerical 3 @ $12,000	36,000
	$162,000

Overhead Expense Budget (Facilities):

Rent including insurance, janitorial and maintenance	$48,000
Depreciation of furniture, fixtures, equipment, and leasehold items	27,000
Utilities	10,000
	$85,000

Overhead Expense Budget:

Advertising	$10,000
Supplies	5,000
Other	4,000
	$19,000

ABC Company Operating Plan
for the Year 2000—*continued*

Operating Income Budget:	
Sales	$400,000
Operating costs	
Merchandise	54,000
Salaries	162,000
Facilities	85,000
Administrative/promotion	19,000
Total cost of sales	320,000
Operating income	$80,000
Cash Flow Budget:	
Operating income	$80,000
Interest expense	15,000
Income before taxes	65,000
Income taxes	10,000
Net income	$55,000
Add: depreciation	27,000
Deduct: debt payment	0
Net cash flow	$82,000

After the operating plan is completed, various budgets to forecast anticipated revenue and expenses streams can be completed. These budgets are used to compare actual versus planned performance in the months (year) ahead.

KEY 13

The first year of operations is an important time for a new enterprise

The first year of operations is an important time for a new enterprise. The entrepreneur must work diligently during this period in order to make plans become realities. In the first year, revenues may be less than forecasted amounts and the company may have only enough cash to support a few months of operations. If the enterprise is fortunate and revenues grow more rapidly than expected, the entrepreneur may have difficulty controlling the levels of accounts receivable and inventories. Growth in both of these items may cause the company to exceed its financial capacities. Moreover, a supposedly profitable company may only be profitable from an accounting standpoint. All the profits may show up in receivables (that may not be collected) or inventories (that may not be sold). For the first year in any case, it is cash in the bank and not accounting profit that the entrepreneur should focus on. As a consequence, planning for the first year of operations must be done in detail.

For the enterprise to survive, it will be necessary to develop detailed budgets for revenues, production, expenses and cash flow. Depending on what type of business is created, these budgets may be needed by month, by week, or even by day. Operational and financial surprises can doom a new company and the entrepreneur cannot wait until the end of the first fiscal quarter to ascertain the condition of the business. Firms that sell big-ticket items, such as automobile dealerships, large appliance dealers and home-builders will not gain much from a daily or weekly budgeting and control system. Alternatively, a restaurant may find itself in serious financial jeopardy if the owner does not have knowledge of daily meals served from the first day of operations. In general, if a company's sales may vary significantly from day-to-day, the firm should prepare daily budgets and daily operating statements. Depending on the type of company, the new organization should construct the following budgets:

♦ A monthly (weekly, daily) marketing (sales) budget

♦ A monthly (weekly, daily) production budget

♦ A monthly (weekly, daily) purchases budget

♦ A monthly (weekly, daily) personnel budget

♦ A monthly (weekly, daily) overhead budget

♦ A monthly (weekly, daily) operating income budget

♦ A monthly (weekly, daily) cash flow budget

- A monthly (weekly, daily) cash balance budget

- A monthly (weekly, daily) financing budget

In some situations, the business may not need to create all of the types of budgets; while in other instances, even more detailed information than that specified above may be needed. The budgets that are prepared for the first fiscal year should be based on the operating plan that was created for the complete business plan. For the car wash business (ABC Company), daily budgets should be prepared.

KEY 14

Growth strategies may be affected by the goals and objectives of the business

Growth strategies may be affected by the goals and objectives of the business. Previously in this book we indicated that a key starting point in the business planning process was the specification of broad (narrative) goals and specific (quantitative or numerical) objectives for the business venture. This was true because different goals/objectives require different strategies.

A firm can establish any number of goals/objectives. However, certain goals/objectives may conflict with other goals/objectives. The primary reason for formally positing goals and objectives is to preclude the pursuit of strategies designed to achieve mutually exclusive (or conflicting) goals. Therefore it is appropriate to have a primary goal (such as public service) as long as it acknowledged that this goal *might* be inconsistent with a second goal (say, of constructing a highly profitable company). Non-economic goals are quite appropriate and may be included in the business plan. However, the entrepreneur should remember that economic goals normally are important goals, if not the most important, in business planning. Furthermore, almost every economic goal relates to the growth of the enterprise.

Growth objectives vary among businesses. A growth strategy that is attractive for one enterprise may be completely inappropriate to another. To assess what growth strategies are feasible, the entrepreneur must re-examine the external and internal factors that were enumerated when the complete business plan was prepared (discussed in Key 8).

Every entrepreneur has his or her own reason for desiring to grow the enterprise and his or her own methods for achieving growth. Each company has a specific set of growth determinants that differs from other firms. The factors that lead to growth for one company will not necessarily work in another enterprise. Even with the uniqueness of firms, however, there are some broad determinants that will be of importance to many companies. For example, overall economic activity such as housing starts, consumer expenditures, business investment and inflation rate may be salient variables impacting many types of businesses. Furthermore, internal variables may be applicable. Examples of such internal variables that may be significant determinants of a company's revenue growth pattern include marketing strategy, promotion policies, product pricing and distribution methods.

Profit growth is influenced by many of the same factors that determine revenue growth. As might be expected, larger sales volume is frequently the most important reason for profit growth. Given that the equation for computing profit includes cost, then efforts to control expenses can also contribute to net income growth. Thus, even if there is a constant or declining sales volume, profit may increase if the cost of goods sold, selling expenses, administrative expenses and other costs of doing business are reduced accordingly.

Let all your things have their places; let each part of your business have its time.

Benjamin Franklin, **Autobiography**

KEY 15

There is no law that requires a business to grow

When the entrepreneur develops long-range goals and objectives beyond the first year in business, she needs to think about the role growth should play in the future of the company. Remember that there is no requirement that a business must grow. In fact, because some entrepreneurs do not want the managerial, administrative and other problems that accompany a big business, they actively resist growth.

Most people, however, get bored doing the same thing day after day and year after year. Growth and change seem to go together and remove the boredom. Moreover, the stimulation and rewards (financial and otherwise) that accompany organizational growth tend to motivate the best employees of a company, who may move to other companies if their job responsibilities become too moribund. Furthermore, there is some truth in the old saying that if an enterprise wants to survive it must grow. Without some forward momentum, it may become lethargic in other ways than financial. Thus, the entrepreneur must reflect on growth strategies very thoughtfully.

When an enterprise grows, so does risk. When a larger company makes a mistake, it is usually more expensive than the same mistake made by a smaller firm. However, the larger company may

The growth of large

business is merely survival

of the fittest.

John D. Rockefeller,
Social Darwinism in American Thought

be in a better position because of its size to absorb the consequences. As a company grows, the influence of bankers, other creditors and additional stake holders is likely to increase and the entrepreneur may lose control of the organization.

The entrepreneurial skills necessary to start a company and stave off disaster in the early years are not necessarily those required to run a complicated managerial organization. In some situations, the entrepreneur may become detrimental to the business and be forced to step aside and appoint professional managers to operate the firm. For many business owners, this price for growth may not be worth it. On the other hand, it may be more attractive to many entrepreneurs to own, say, 15 percent of a large publicly held corporation with stock worth many millions of dollars than to own all of an illiquid business that can, at best, pay its owners a good salary.

It is not the intention of this book to provide entrepreneurs with sets of goals and objectives. However, it is important to note that one strategy followed successfully by many entrepreneurs is that of adopting a conservative growth posture. That is, growth for its own sake is avoided as a strategy, and the firm is encouraged to grow when business conditions, financing and opportunities permit.

KEY 16

Simple growth calculations are easy to make and should be a focal point for the entrepreneur

I n their simplest format, growth calculations are merely the ratios of two (or more) numbers expressed for a specific time horizon. Therefore, if ABC Company had sales of $400,000 in 2000 and $500,000 in 2001, then the growth rate for the company would be: ($500,000 − $400,000)/$400,000 = 25% during the one year period. A convenient formula that can be used to express the growth relationship is:

$$G = \frac{X_1 - X_0}{X_0}$$

Where:

 G is the growth rate for the period in question

 X_1 is the value of the variable at the end of the period in question

 X_0 is the value of the variable at the beginning of the period in question

When using the formula it makes no difference whether the time period is months, years or days. Longer periods of time, such as two years, three years or more can be utilized. Growth rates can also be calculated for variables that are recorded at some point in time such as asset and liability categories. As an example, ABC Company, Inc. might compare from 2000 to 2001 the growth in inventory. Suppose that as of January 1, 2000, inventory was $5,000, and as of December 31, 2000, it was $6,000. Then the growth rate of inventory for the year would be ($6,000 − $5,000) / ($5,000) = 20%.

As illustrated above, growth rates can be calculated for periods of time that have already occurred. Growth rates can also be useful for future business planning. For example, it may be more convenient to express specific financial objectives using growth rates rather than actual numbers. Suppose ABC Company earned $55,000 in profits during 2000. Then the operating plan for 2001 might project that earnings will increase by 18.2 percent. Stated as dollar profits, the planned growth is ($0.182 \times \$55,000$) = $10,000 and the value of dollar profits would be [$55,000 + (0.182 \times \$55,000$)] ≈ $65,000.

The basic growth relationship formula specified above can be rewritten to solve for the value of the variable at the end of the time period in question:

$$X_1 = X_0 (1 + G)$$

Therefore, the value for the variable at the end of the period can be obtained by multiplying the value at the beginning of the period by one plus the growth rate. Using the example above $X_1 = (\$55,000)(1.182) = \$65,010$.

When calculations go beyond the one-period case, they are somewhat more complicated and require the use of the simpler equations as a foundation. Computations involving more than one period are completed on what is called a compounded basis. Thus, if ABC Company had $55,000 in profits in 2000, and desired to have earnings increase by 18.2 percent per year for the next five years, then planned profit for 2005 would be:

$$X_{2001} = (\$55,000)(1.182) = \$65,010$$
$$X_{2002} = (\$65,010)(1.182) = \$76,842$$
$$X_{2003} = (\$76,842)(1.182) = \$90,827$$
$$X_{2004} = (\$90,827)(1.182) = \$107,358$$
$$X_{2005} = (\$107,358)(1.182) = \$126,897$$

Note, all that has been done is to repeat the basic growth relationship:

$$X_1 = X_0 (1 + G)$$

several times. Since this process is cumbersome, it is fortunate that there is a simpler procedure available. This method is based on a rearrangement of the simple formula as follows:

$$X_n = X_0 (1 + G)^n$$

Therefore, for the numerical example given above, the profit objective after the first year could be computed as follows:

$$X_1 = X_0(1 + 0.182)^1$$

$$X_{2001} = (\$55,000)(1 + 0.182)^1 = (\$55,000)(1.182) = \$65,010$$

and the objective after the second year as:

$$X_2 = X_0(1 + G)^2$$

$$X_{2002} = (\$55,000)(1 + 0.182)^2 = (\$55,000)(1.397) =$$
$$\$76,835$$

By analogy, the following may be determined:

$$X_3 = X_0 (1 + G)^3$$
$$X_4 = X_0 (1 + G)^4$$
$$X_5 = X_0 (1 + G)^5$$

or, in general

$$X_n = X_0 (1 + G)^n$$

For the example above after 5 years, we would find:

$$X_{2005} = (\$55,000)(1 + 0.182)^5 = (\$55,000)(2.30722) =$$
$$\$126,897$$

Prior to the days of inexpensive hand-held calculators or personal computers, these growth calculations were made with compound interest tables. Today, a personal computer or calculator may be used to make the computations. The use of these machines saves a great deal of time, but the entrepreneur still needs to know the arithmetic that lies behind the computations. Otherwise, they tend to become meaningless.

KEY 17

Growth calculations may be expanded to include return on investment (R.O.I.) analysis

The simple growth calculations shown in Key 16 may be expanded to include return on investment, or R.O.I., analysis. Generally, an enterprise must acquire and deploy assets to produce a product or service. While the investments may be in fixed assets such as property, plant and equipment, the amount of dollars in current assets should also be considered. For many companies the amount of capital invested in receivables, inventories and cash may be an important determinant of R.O.I. As noted previously, revenue growth is probably the most important factor for profit growth. Furthermore, the most significant determinant for improving R.O.I. is profit growth. However, even when profits are decreasing, an enterprise can increase its return on investment by reducing the volume of assets necessary to create sales.

Finance textbooks have utilized a simple equation to evaluate and analyze R.O.I. for a long time. The formula includes the major determinants of

R.O.I. and can be helpful in demonstrating why a company's investment returns are rising or falling. The formula is:

$$R.O.I. = \frac{\text{Net income}}{\text{Total assets}} = \frac{\text{Sales}}{\text{Total assets}} \times \frac{\text{Net income}}{\text{Sales}}$$

Therefore, R.O.I. is defined as the ratio of net income (profit) to the total assets invested in the enterprise. This ratio is really the product of two other ratios. The first determinant ratio is the asset turnover ratio, which is computed by dividing sales by total assets. The second ratio is the net margin ratio which is calculated by dividing net income by sales. Thus, there are two ways for the entrepreneur to improve R.O.I.: either generate more sales per dollar of asset investment or increase the profit margin on each dollar of sales.

Let's examine the R.O.I. formula in the case of the car wash business discussed earlier in this book (ABC Company). Recall that the sales expectation for ABC in the year 2000 was $400,000, the expected net income was $55,000, and the total asset investment in the business was $250,000. We could immediately calculate ABC's expected R.O.I. as: $55,000/$250,000 = 22.00%. This return could be broken down into its asset turnover component (Sales/total assets) or ($400,000/$250,000 = 1.6), and its profit margin component (Net income/sales) or ($55,000/ $400,000 = 13.75%). Multiplying the asset turnover (1.6) by the profit margin (13.75%) results in the return on investment for ABC, or (1.6) × (13.75%) = 22%.

KEY 18

Long-term growth may depend on the ability to get long-term financing

O nce the entrepreneur has specified a growth strategy, he must determine how to finance the growth. Essentially, there are two principal ways to finance growth: (1) internally generated funds and (2) funds obtained from external financial sources. In the financial literature, the distinction is also often made between *gross* and *net* sources. All the funds available to finance the firm's operations from operating income, depreciation flows, other non-cash charges and asset conversions are considered gross internal sources.

Net sources are those funds available after depreciating assets are replenished and all payments are made to the government (taxes) and suppliers of funds. The primary source of internal funds is from retained earnings, because depreciation flows are usually utilized to replenish fixed assets. Dividend and interest payments that are paid to suppliers of funds and income tax payments to the government are taken from operating or other non-operating sources.

New enterprises should be careful and not concentrate too much on net internal sources of financing. In early stages, a well-planned company should have ample funds. Therefore, the timing of fixed asset replacement may be more important than the fact that such assets must be replaced eventually. This situation is one prominent reason for focusing on net rather than gross sources of finance. In most situations, new companies purchase fixed assets immediately that may not require replacement for several years. Prior to replacement, the depreciation expenses for the fixed assets that are allocated on the income statement are actually sources of funds to continue the operations of the business.

Unfortunately, if the business loses money for several years, the retained earnings remain negative and the firm will not be able to replace its operating assets. Without funds to replace the operating assets, the enterprise may be forced to cease operations. The entrepreneur must remember that if the company is growing, then it is more probable that accounts receivables and inventories will be *increasing* instead of contracting and therefore these asset categories will be a *use* of finance instead of a source. As the company continues to operate over a series of years, fixed assets may become a use instead of a source of funds. A growing company will probably add to its fixed assets at a faster rate than the fixed assets are depreciated. In this situation, financial resources from depreciation may be insufficient and not available to finance other requirements for the enterprise. External secured funds may be utilized by the enterprise. The use of external funds may be necessary for two reasons: (1) internal funds are not sufficient to finance the growth of the company, or (2) funds can be obtained at very attractive rates and the business owner decides to use external funds instead of internal funds. Typically, external financial sources are considered to be either short-term or long-term. Supplier credit, bank loans, commercial finance and receivables factoring are examples of short-term financial sources.

Long-term financing sources include incurring long-term debt with financial intermediaries such as banks or insurance companies, leasing and the sale of equity through common and preferred stock issuances. A financial source is considered long-term if repayment occurs more than one year in the future.

I have always recognized that the object of business is to make money in an honorable manner.

Peter Cooper

KEY 19

Operating leverage is a key element in determining the riskiness of a business

When a company has a volatile sales pattern, it lacks a sure inflow of cash. Such a situation has two distinct disadvantages: (1) the firm may not be able to meet its cash payment obligations on a timely basis, and (2) a risky pattern of cash flows will usually result in an unstable income pattern. In the first situation, the possibility of insolvency increases, and in the second situation the variability may reduce the value of the business.

Even though revenue predictability is the most important factor in evaluating the risk level for a business, other variables may increase the impact resulting from a volatile cash flow pattern. One example of such a variable is the degree of operating leverage characteristic of the firm. High operating fixed costs are inherent to a firm having a high degree of operating leverage. Examples of operating fixed costs include items such as depreciation, overhead and permanent salaries. If a company has high operating fixed costs, then the possibility of insolvency increases because fixed costs do not change with output volume. As a result, the volatility of earnings increases. Items like depreciation, which are not cash charges, may impact earnings volatility, but do not increase the probability of the firm's running short of cash.

Business is like riding a bicycle. Either you keep moving or you fall down.

John David Wright, The Road to Diversity

Assume the ABC Company (our car wash example) has completed its research and analysis and determined the following set of sales possibilities for the year 2000:

	Sales
Maximum expectation	$500,000
Most likely expectation	400,000
Minimum expectation	300,000

Furthermore, assume that the business has a variable cost ratio (variable cost/sales) of 0.5 and operating fixed costs of $120,000. In the best of all possible worlds, where sales are $500,000, the firm's income statement would be as follows:

Sales		$500,000
Variable costs	$250,000	
Operating fixed costs	120,000	370,000
Operating income		$130,000

If sales are only $400,000, however, the operating income would be:

Sales		$400,000
Variable costs	$200,000	
Operating fixed costs	120,000	320,000
Operating income		$80,000

In the worst of all possible worlds, where sales are $300,000:

Sales		$300,000
Variable costs	$150,000	
Operating fixed costs	120,000	270,000
Operating income		$ 30,000

Thus, the presence of operating fixed costs in the third instance would result in only $30,000 in operating income for the firm. Put another way, a swing of 25 percent ($400,000 ± $100,000) results in an operating income fluctuation of 62.5 percent ($80,000 ± $50,000).

KEY 20

Deciding when and how the business reaches the break-even point is critical to its success

A company's operating leverage is often analyzed by using break-even analysis. The break-even point is specified as the level of sales where expenses exactly equal sales. A company with no fixed costs has a break-even sales point of zero. The variable cost ratio is an important factor in break-even analysis, because a firm's contribution to fixed costs (and profit in excess of the break-even point) is dependent on how much of each additional dollar of sales is used to cover variable costs. For the example in Key 19, the variable cost ratio for the ABC Company is assumed to be 0.5. Therefore the contribution to cover fixed costs and profit for each additional dollar of sales is $0.50. Thus, sales must be $240,000 in the case of a fixed cost level of $120,000 for the organization to break even. For every dollar of sales less than $240,000, then the firm incurs an operating loss of $0.50. On the flip side, there is an operating profit of $0.50 for every dollar of sales in excess of $240,000.

The following equation specifies these relationships:

$$S_b = \frac{FC}{1 - \dfrac{VC}{S}}$$

Where:

    S_b is break-even sales

    FC is the value of operating fixed costs

    VC is the variable cost per unit of sales

    S is the selling price per unit

The variable cost ratio can be determined in two ways. One alternative is to divide the variable cost per unit (assume $4 per unit for ABC) by the selling price per unit (assume $8 per unit). The unit expression drops out and the VC is 0.5. A second method for calculating the VC ratio is by dividing the total variable costs appearing on the income statement by total sales appearing on the income statement. To explore the importance of operating leverage on the riskiness of a company in more detail, let us consider another example. Suppose that ABC has a high degree of operating leverage. Assume that $VC/S = 0.8$ and operating fixed costs remain at $120,000. Then the break-even point (sales value) would be:

$$S_b = \frac{\$120,000}{1 - 0.8} = \$600,000$$

Thus, the break-even point for the ABC Company would be much higher. In fact, even with the most optimistic sales level of $500,000, the car wash could not break even.

KEY 21

Trade credit is often overlooked as a key source of short-term financing

The ability of a firm to get financing depends on its relative riskiness (see discussion in Keys 19 and 20). Fortunately, even the riskiest enterprise can often get short-term financing with little or no trouble. Suppliers may be an important source of this sort of short-term finance, and an often overlooked fact is that employees provide useful services between paychecks! Thus, they provide a free source of short-term funds. For example, if ABC begins its car wash operation on a Monday, chances are it will not have to make a payroll until at least the end of the week. For this period of time, ABC's employees have helped finance the business.

Assuming that a company earns a profit during a quarter, the government may also be a free supplier source of finance. This is because company income tax payments are due on a quarterly basis. Of course, money withheld from paychecks for employee social security and personal income tax purposes must be remitted much more frequently,

Bad business practices, if left uncorrected, will drive out good business practices.

Ralph Nader, **Public Citizen Number One**

and the wise employer will never consider these funds as a company source of finance. Many small (and not so small) entrepreneurs have been tempted to use payroll tax deposit dollars for operating purposes rather than remitting them to the government. Sadly, nothing will get a business closed down faster by the Internal Revenue Service than this practice, and it should be avoided at all costs.

The primary source of supplier financing is through trade credit. A supplier grants trade credit to a company when the company is not required to make payment prior to or at the time of delivery for materials, merchandise, or other items. Sometimes a supplier may sell its products to a company on terms net/10, E.O.M. This term means that payment for purchase made during a month is due 10 days after the end of the month. Therefore, the company is provided short-term funds for as few as 10 days or as many as 40 days. These funds are provided at no specified cost. However, a case can be made that the supplier includes this cost in the selling price for its goods or services.

Sometimes trade credit is issued with a discount. For example, supplier terms of 2/10, net 30 mean that if the company completes payment within 10 days, then the supplier will discount the invoice value by 2 percent. Assuming that less expensive sources of finance are available, the shrewd entrepreneur will pay within 10 days. Should the business owner not pay within 10 days, then she should take the full 30 days to pay. Otherwise the entrepreneur would not take advantage of an essentially free source of funds. If the discount is not taken, the cost can be computed as follows:

PERCENTAGE DISCOUNT

$$\frac{\% \text{ discount}}{100\% - \% \text{ discount}} \times \frac{365}{\text{Total period} - \text{Discount period}}$$

In the case of terms "2/10, net 30," the annualized cost of funds would be:

$$\frac{2\%}{98\%} \times \frac{365}{20} = 37.2\%$$

Suppose an invoice for $800 was presented to the ABC Company for car wash supplies. Only ($800) × (0.98) = $784 is due if the company pays the invoice within 10 days. The full $800 would be due in 30 days. The savings of $16 is the cost of using $784 for 20 more days. Dividing 20 days into 365 (or, 365/20 = 18.25), the ABC Company can annualize the 20-day use of funds such that the cost of funds is:

$$\frac{\$16}{\$784} \times 18.25 = (0.0204)(18.25) = 37.2\%$$

Of course, business owners should make payment by the end of the assigned 30-day period. Some firms may not pay on time. This policy, which is sometimes called stretching payables, is utilized by companies that are weak and in a cash-deficient position or by many businesses during times of tight money in the economy. Such operational tactics may lead to a lowering of the enterprise's credit rating. When a firm's credit rating deteriorates for any reason, its suppliers become more reluctant to sell to the company on credit. It is difficult to quantify the cost of a deteriorated credit rating, but it can be substantial. If there is going to be a delay in paying a supplier, it is smart to explain why and state when the payment should be expected.

KEY 22

Bank financing may be available to certain businesses

Another major source of short-term funds that may be available to an enterprise is bank credit. This funding source is usually fairly inexpensive. Hence, it is particularly important for entrepreneurs to devote appropriate amounts of time developing good banking relationships. If a company has good planning processes, the entrepreneur will meet with bankers on financing needs long before the actual date that funds are needed. Unfortunately, too often business owners do not practice this principle. Well-managed companies also keep minimum balances at their bank. Such a practice is a good precursor for creating a solid banking relationship. Business owners should provide their bank with periodic company financial statements. Since a bank often asks that the business owner be personally liable for a bank loan to his business, it is also a good idea to provide the bank with a personal financial statement.

By satisfying the prerequisites outlined above, the

entrepreneur may be able to establish a line of credit with the bank. Such an agreement indicates that the bank will lend the enterprise up to a given amount of money at a specified interest rate. The interest rate applicable to such a loan is usually tied to the current prime rate (the rate charged to borrowers having the best credit-worthiness). For example, an entrepreneur might be charged prime plus 1 percent. To demonstrate the liquidity of a business, the bank may require the company to owe the bank nothing for some period during the year. This requirement is called the clean-up provision. While a line of credit is useful to the entrepreneur, it is not legally binding on the bank. In fact, the bank can significantly reduce the amount of credit at any time and may likely do so during periods of tight credit.

To reduce the risk of having the amount of the line of credit reduced, the entrepreneur can enter a more formal credit arrangement with the bank. A revolving credit guarantee is a binding commitment for the bank to lend a company up to a given amount at a specified interest rate for a stated period of time, typically a year. As was the case for a line of credit, the interest rate is usually tied to the prime rate.

One way the bank can remove itself from this commitment is if the company's financial situation deteriorates. The bank can also refuse to honor the commitment if credit conditions tighten. For providing the credit guarantee, the bank will normally require a fee. This fee is often 0.5 percent per year or more, and it is paid on the unborrowed balance. For example, assume that the ABC Company has a $300,000 revolving credit arrangement at prime plus 1.5 percent with 0.5 percent being paid on the unborrowed balance. Suppose further that ABC has average borrowings of $150,000 during the year. Assuming the prime rate averages 8 percent during the period, the total cost of the revolving credit arrangement with the bank is:

$$(\$150,000)(0.095) + (\$150,000)(0.005) = \$15,000$$

Since the average amount borrowed during the year was $150,000, the cost of finance would be:

$$(\$15,000)/\$150,000 = 10\%$$

When an entrepreneur requests a loan, the bankers will examine closely his bank balances. Bankers typically will loan to their own depositors as opposed to a non-depositor.

Making short-term loans on the current assets of small companies is one type of loan that some banks and commercial finance companies specialize in making. It is often possible for an enterprise to borrow from 50 percent to 80 percent of the face value of accounts receivable and 30 percent to 60 percent of inventory cost. When a bank handles the collection of the accounts receivable an additional fee of 1 percent to 2 percent is also charged. If the entrepreneur borrows from a commercial finance company, the interest rate may be significantly higher. Whenever possible, entrepreneurs prefer to borrow on a non-notification basis. Under this arrangement, the business owner continues to collect the receivable without the customer knowing that the enterprise has borrowed against the receivable. Of course the lender would prefer that the receivable be paid directly to it.

Financing through banks for new companies is often not available. Banks are not in the venture capital business. Any loans provided to brand new firms are usually based on the income and personal assets of the individual entrepreneur rather than his company. Even if the new enterprise is a corporation, the entrepreneur will usually have to personally guarantee any loans to the new company. Therefore, the bank will expect payments from the entrepreneur in case the business has problems.

KEY 23

Factoring may be an important source of funds available to a new business

An enterprise can also sell its receivables to a factor. The advantage to the company of factoring is that it may no longer have to have a credit department with its related costs or incur bad debt losses. The factoring company agrees to assume these responsibilities if the receivables are sold under a "non-recourse" basis. The factoring company purchases the receivables and then collects all funds and takes the risk of non-payment by customers.

For providing the abovementioned service, the factor charges a fee, usually about 2 percent of the receivables purchased, which covers the credit and collection activities. The enterprise that sells its receivables to a factor does not receive any funds until after the factor is paid. If the enterprise wants funds sooner, it may be able to borrow money from the factor at some specific interest rate. If the business elects to keep money on deposit with the factor after the receivables are collected, the factor may pay the company interest on the deposit. To calculate the cost of factoring receivables, several items must be considered: First, the charges of the factoring company for its services must be calculated. Second, the bad debt savings generated if non-recourse factoring is used must be determined. Third, the savings from not maintaining a credit department must be ascertained. And fourth, the interest paid or earned on factored accounts must be computed.

Assume that XYZ Company had credit sales of $300,000 per year and had an average receivables turnover of 5 times per year (every 73 days). Therefore, the average amount of receivables maintained by XYZ would be $300,000/5 or $60,000. If a factor would lend XYZ 80 percent of its outstanding receivables, charged a fee of 2 percent on the total volume of receivables factored, and required the payment of 18 percent interest on any funds advanced to XYZ, then the gross cost for the factoring would be:

$$(0.02)(\$300,000) + (0.18)(\$48,000) = \$14,640$$

If XYZ had a typical bad debt write off of ½ percent of sales and would have to spend $3,000 on credit evaluations and collections, its savings would be:

$$(0.005)(\$300,000) + \$3,000 = \$4,500$$

Thus, the net cost of factoring would be:

$$\$14,640 - \$4,500 = \$10,140 \text{ or:}$$
$$\$10,140/\$48,000 = 21.125\%$$

When a business is able to sell its receivables to a factor without recourse, then the factor has the right to approve the credit worthiness of the company's customers. As might be expected, the factor will take a more conservative approach in evaluating the customers to which the company sells. The approach may to lead to lost sales to some customers by the marketing department because the factor may not be willing to extend credit to some customers.

Work smarter, not harder.

Ron Carswell, Carswell Law of Productivity

KEY 24

Selling common stock to outsiders may be a big mistake

The first financing source for a new company is usually the sale of common stock. Of course, proprietorships and partnerships do not sell stock, but rather have owners' equity or partners' capital. Nevertheless, the basic concepts are similar. In the case of an entrepreneur who incorporates, the entrepreneur usually purchases the first shares of common stock to provide the initial money for the company. If the entrepreneur sells stock to other people to raise funds, then the entrepreneur is essentially bringing new partners into the company.

In some situations the inclusion of additional stockholders may be a good idea while in others it may not. Selling stock to other people can be the biggest mistake ever made by the entrepreneur. For one thing, the entrepreneur's equity holdings are diluted when she sells stock to others. Furthermore, minority stockholders can be a nuisance to the company and to the entrepreneur. In some situations, they may actually file lawsuits against the company and/or the entrepreneur. On the positive side, the entrepreneur may not be able to raise funds in any other manner. Also, by having more equity in the enterprise, it may be easier to borrow money. Thus, as a result of raising funds from selling stock to others, the company may have the ability to obtain substantially more money than otherwise would be the case.

As we noted earlier in this book, earnings retained each year are the primary source of finance for an enterprise that has gotten beyond the startup stage and is profitable. Assuming the company is profitable, then retaining earnings is the easiest source of finance to utilize. There are no formalities such as loan agreements, bond indentures and warrant agreements to worry about. To retain earnings, all the board of directors must do is refrain from paying out all of the firm's earnings in dividends. Since there are very few instances when a privately held company that is growing should pay a substantial dividend anyway, it is easy to automatically retain earnings.

Although the decision to go public is beyond the scope of this book, the business owner who really wants his firm to grow may be able to do so only by going public. If the entrepreneur decides to go public, however, she must be careful to file any required documents with the Securities and Exchange Commission and to comply with state laws. The entrepreneur may also be required to significantly dilute her position when shares are sold to the public. In addition, it is common for the legal, accounting and underwriting costs required to take a firm public to absorb 20 percent to 30 percent of the total proceeds of the stock offering. Thus the enterprise is left with only 70 percent to 80 percent of the stock offering proceeds.

On the other hand, if a company wants to grow rapidly, going public is one of the best ways to do so. Furthermore, by going public, entrepreneurs may get to be millionaires quicker by than by remaining privately held. In addition, by having shares traded in the public market, the entrepreneur may improve her liquidity and establish a value for the most important asset she owns.

A business with an income at its heels furnishes always oil for its own wheels.

Cowper, Retirement

Publicly traded stock is also easier to use as collateral for personal loans. As another bonus, the entrepreneur may be able to leave his or her heirs in a far better financial situation by bequeathing them public stock rather than stock in a private company. It is much easier for heirs to pay estate and inheritance taxes by liquidating some public stock than trying to sell a privately held enterprise.

If the entrepreneur sells some of her publicly held stock while she is still alive, the individual can diversify her personal portfolio. Finally, as we noted earlier, it may be more beneficial for the entrepreneur to own 20 percent of a public corporation worth $150 million than own all of the stock in a privately held company having a value of $2 million.

Still, the decision to go public shouldn't be made lightly. Once you take that step, it can be difficult or impossible to take your company private again. Before acting, obviously, you should seek professional advice.

KEY 25

Venture capital is not available for most entrepreneurs, but it can be attractive for the few that qualify

Venture capitalists are individuals or institutions that invest in entrepreneurial situations. Although most start-up businesses do not qualify for venture capital funding, a few that offer unique growth opportunities may raise capital from this source. Venture capital will be more likely made available to companies that have been around for awhile and are seeking growth capital.

Venture capitalists are professionals who often bring managerial and financial expertise to the enterprise. The biggest disadvantage of raising venture capital (aside from the obvious dilution impact) is that the entrepreneur may lose control of the business at some point to his or her financial backers.

Venture capital investment may take several forms. Often, a venture capitalist will lend money to the entrepreneurial firm. When a venture capitalist lends money, he still expects to get some form of equity participation in the business. Many prefer to receive warrants as their kicker. The venture capitalist can then use the warrant, which is a legal instrument much like an option, to purchase shares of stock at a given price.

Thus, a venture capitalist may be willing to loan an entrepreneurial concern, say, $500,000. At the same time, the venture capitalist requires the entrepreneur to provide warrants to purchase, say, 100,000 shares of common stock at $5 per share. In this case, the venture capitalist would eventually have the loan repaid, receiving $500,000 in cash. He would then exercise the right provided by the warrants to purchase stock. In some cases, venture capitalists will ask for warrants to allow the purchase of stock at nominal prices. For example, a venture capitalist might be willing to lend a company $500,000, but it also expects to receive the right to purchase, say, 100,000 shares at $0.10 per share. The venture capitalist would ultimately receive the funds from the loan repayment but would still secure an equity stake at a low price. In the example, 100,000 shares would be received for a total cost of $10,000.

Long-term lenders such as insurance companies often assume a venture-capital role and ask for an opportunity to participate in the growth of the borrowing company. One way the enterprise can allow a lender such a growth opportunity is to grant the lender the right to purchase some common stock (as in the warrant case discussed above). Another possibility would be to make the debt instrument convertible into common stock. Convertible securities include an option that allows the lender to tender the convertible debt (or preferred stock, see below) and exchange it for common shares. For example, suppose a lender purchased $500,000 of ABC Company's 12 percent notes due in 2010. Assume there is an option that allows the notes to be converted into 100,000 shares of ABC common stock at $5 per share. The conversion ratio specifies the number of common stock shares obtained by the lender if the note is converted. If the ABC Company's notes were issued in the form of $1,000 par value bonds, then each note would be convertible into 200 shares of stock. The conversion price is the par value of the bond divided by the conversion ratio. For the ABC Company, Inc. notes, the conversion price would be $1,000/200 = $5. Preferred stock is an equity instrument that is occasionally purchased by venture capitalists and other long-term investors.

Preferred stock includes a combination of the features of debt and common stock. Preferred stock is similar to common stock in that it is called stock and it appears in the equity section on the balance sheet. Furthermore, payments to preferred stock holders are considered dividends and are therefore not deductible for income tax purposes. Other similarities of preferred stock and common stock include the fact that dividend payments may not be required on either and both typically have no maturity date.

There are types of preferred stock that differ from common stock. For example, cumulative preferred stock allows for the non-payment of dividends but typically requires the accumulation and payment of all prior due payments (called dividends in arrears) before any common dividends can be paid. This form of preferred stock also often allows its holders as a class to elect some (or even all) of the board of directors of the company in the event that dividends are passed (not paid) for a given period of time.

Preferred stock is like debt in that, if a dividend is

declared, there is usually a fixed (rather than participating or variable) rate paid. There is a form of preferred stock called participating preferred where the dividend can vary (as with a common stock dividend) depending on the prosperity of the company, but it is rarely used. There is also a type of preferred stock, called redeemable preferred, that allows a time period when the stock may be repurchased on given terms by the issuer. This form of preferred also often requires the issuer to redeem (pay off) all of the issue at some point.

When venture capital financing is a possibility for an enterprise, the question frequently arises as to what percentage of the deal the venture capitalist should receive for providing funding. One procedure to determine this percentage is to use the "venture capital method." This process uses an assumed rate of return that the venture capitalist needs to earn to compensate for risks assumed. Thus, the rate depends on the development stage of the enterprise. A venture capitalist demands a higher rate of return on seed and start-up financing than for companies that are already operational and making a profit.

The venture capital method is summarized below:

◆ A company's net income is projected in a business plan for some terminal year, say five years from the present.

◆ A price earnings ratio is determined that is deemed appropriate for a company that has achieved the success implicit in the forecasted income.

◆ A terminal value is calculated by taking the product of the price earnings ratio and terminal year net income.

- ◆ The venture capitalist's required rate of return (r) and investment at the end of the five-year term are determined.

- ◆ The venture capitalist's ownership percentage is then calculated by dividing the value of the venture capitalist's investment at the end of the five-year term by the projected terminal value.

Suppose the owner of ABC Company is able to attract the interest of a venture capitalist. Using the *pro forma* projections appearing in Key 10, the net income in the fifth year is $110,000. Assume that an appropriate price earnings ratio for a successful car wash operation is 10. Then the terminal value of the business at the end of five years is $1,100,000

For this example, assume that the entrepreneur will obtain $75,000 from the venture capitalist and will invest $25,000 of his own money. Since the car wash is an established type of business and the entrepreneur is in the start-up phase, we shall assume an appropriate rate of return for the venture capitalist is 50 percent. This means that the value of the venture capitalist's investment at the end of the terminal year is calculated by multiplying $75,000 times $(1 + 0.5)^5 = \$75,000 \times 7.59375 = \$569,531$.

Therefore, at the end of the five-year period, the venture capitalist will have to have $569,531 in order to have earned a 50 percent compounded annual return. This would represent 51.8 percent of the total value of the enterprise $(\$569,531/\$1,100,000) = $ 51.8 percent in year 5. Put another way, the venture capitalist would have to own 51.8 percent of the business to achieve her return objective, given the business plan projection of ABC Company, Inc.

Note that a venture capitalist is typically not interested in long-term ownership of an enterprise. Therefore, he is always interested in knowing the exit strategies planned by the entrepreneur. A venture capitalist is more likely to enter a venture if there is an obvious exit strategy (such as sale of the company or a public stock offering).

A man's success in business today turns upon his power of getting people to believe he has something they want.

Gerald Stanley Lee, **Crowds**

INDEX

AUTHORS

EDWARD E. WILLIAMS, Ph.D., is the Henry Gardiner Symonds Professor and Director of the Entrepreneurship Program in the Jesse H. Jones Graduate School of Administration at Rice University. He is a member of the Board of Directors of several companies and has written extensively for both scholarly and professional journals. His publications include over 40 articles and 6 books, including *Entrepreneurship and Productivity* and *The Economics of Production and Productivity: A Modeling Approach*, and numerous other works. Professor Williams has had the highest teacher evaluation of any professor at Rice University.

JAMES R. THOMPSON, Ph.D., is a Professor of Statistics at the Brown School of Engineering at Rice University. He is a Fellow of the American Statistical Association, the Institute of Mathematical Statistics, and the International Statistical Institute. Dr. Thompson is the winner of the Samuel S. Wilks Medal for his work in Applied Statistics, and is the author of ten books, including *Entrepreneurship, Planning, and Productivity* (with Edward E. Williams), *Simulation: A Modeler's Approach*, and *Empirical Model Building*.

H. ALBERT NAPIER, Ph.D., is a Professor of Management and Psychology in the Jones Graduate School of Management at Rice

University, where he teaches graduate level information technology and entrepreneurship courses. He is also the director of the Center on the Management of Information Technology (COMIT) and is a principal of Napier & Judd, which provides IT consulting and personal computer training services. Dr. Napier is the author of more than 40 books on software applications such as *Office 97*, *Word 97*, *Excel 97*, *Power Point 97*, *Netscape Communicator*, and *Internet Explorer*.